M000107807

PAPER AIRPLANES

PAPER AIRPLANES

Models to Build and Fly

Emery J. Kelly

illustrations by Darren Erickson

photographs by Richard Trombley

Lerner Publications Company • Minneapolis

I dedicate this book to my mother, Ruth I. Kelly, who made my first paper airplane and started me down the road that led to this book.

I also dedicate this book to my children: Mary Mussel, Bill Zeman, Kathy Wojcik, John Zeman, Dan Zeman, and Julie Kasner. They reviewed the book and instructions, then made the airplanes to see that all was understandable.

Words in **bold** type are defined in the glossary on page 64.

Copyright © 1997 by Lerner Publications Company

Second printing 1998

This book is available in two editions:
Library binding by Lerner Publications Company
Soft cover by First Avenue Editions, 2000
Divisions of Lerner Publishing Group
241 First Avenue North
Minneapolis, MN 55401 U.S.A.

All rights reserved. International copyright secured.
No part of this book may be reproduced or transmitted in any form or by any means, electronic or mechanical, including photocopying and recording, or by any information storage or retrieval system, without permission in writing from Lerner Publications Company, except for the inclusion of brief quotations in an acknowledged review.

Website address: www.lernerbooks.com

Library of Congress Cataloging-in-Publication Data

Kelly, Emery J.
    Paper airplanes : models to build and fly / Emery J. Kelly ;
illustrations by Darren Erickson.
        p.   cm.
    Summary: Presents information on aerodynamic principles and flying techniques along with instructions for making twelve different paper airplanes.
    ISBN 0-8225-2401-5 (alk. paper)
    ISBN 0-8225-9903-1 (pbk.)
    1. Paper airplanes—Juvenile literature. [1. Paper airplanes.]
    I. Erickson, Darren, ill. II. Title
TL778.K45   1997
745.592—dc20   96-10909

Manufactured in the United States of America
4 5 6 7 8 9 – JR – 05 04 03 02 01 00

CONTENTS

INTRODUCTION

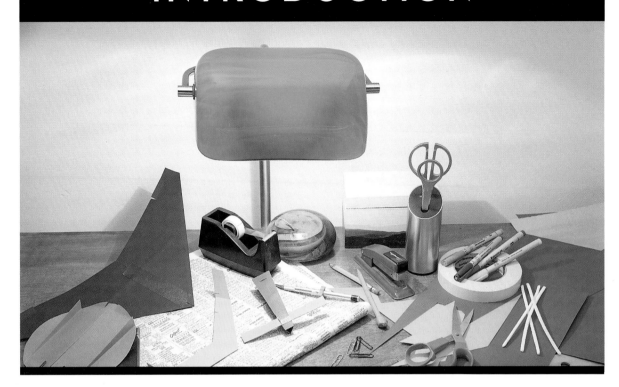

For thousands of years, people have envied birds for their ability to fly. While paper airplanes cannot carry your body into the air, they can help you imagine soaring like the birds. Paper airplanes are easy and inexpensive to construct and they allow you a "flight of fancy" anytime you wish.

MATERIALS

Paper airplanes require little in the way of tools or materials. Most of the airplanes in this book can be built with 15- to 20-pound, 8½-by-11-inch typing paper, tape or staples, and some paper clips. The Ultralight plane uses tissue paper, and the Lilienthal Glider requires pipe cleaners and soldering wire.

You will also need some simple tools, including a ruler, pencil, scissors, a stapler, and an artist's knife with a sharp blade. When using the knife, keep your fingertips away from the blade and out of its cutting path. Also, be sure to protect your work surface with an old magazine or cardboard.

KEY TO DIAGRAMS

The diagrams in this book use different kinds of lines to show how your paper should be cut, folded, or taped.

Dashed lines (— — —) show where to fold the paper.

Solid lines (————) show where paper should be cut.

A short line (— ⊣) across a cut or fold line shows where the fold or cut ends.

▢ shows where to place a piece of tape.

Dot-dashed lines (— · — ·) show the center line of the airplane.

Measurements are shown in inches with the (") symbol. If you are using a metric ruler, multiply the measurement in inches by 2.54 to get centimeters.

CONSTRUCTION TIPS

Most airplanes are symmetrical—that is, the left and right sides are "mirror images" of one another. Instructions for the most complex airplanes in this book have a full-sized drawing of the left half of the airplane. After folding your paper in half and tracing the shape onto the left half, you will cut along the outside lines. In this way, you will cut out the left and right sides of the airplane together. Any extra lines can be copied from the left side of the paper onto the right.

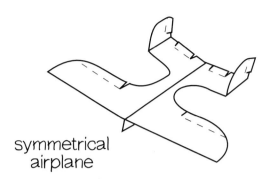

symmetrical airplane

Paper airplanes fly best when the paper is stiff and the folds are sharp. Use a ruler to make your creases straight and sharp. The even, narrow folds needed at the leading edge of many of the airplanes' wings can be made accordion style. Wrap the accordion folds in two final folds to create a smooth edge.

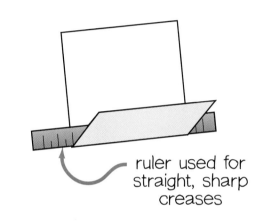

ruler used for straight, sharp creases

During flight and especially after hard landings, paper airplanes may lose their symmetry and balance. You will have to adjust your airplane to keep it in top flying shape. Keep a small roll of tape handy to make quick repairs.

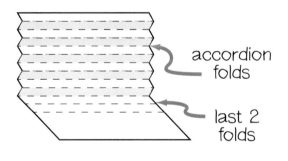

accordion folds

last 2 folds

START SOARING

The first step to flying your paper airplanes, of course, is to gather your materials and get started. If you build the airplanes in the order presented in this book, you will start with simple airplanes and end with a plane that can challenge the most experienced builder/flier. You'll also need some understanding of what makes airplanes fly and how to make yours fly even better.

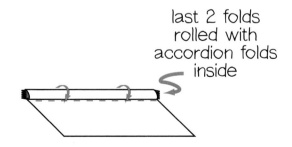

last 2 folds rolled with accordion folds inside

WHAT KEEPS THEM UP?
A Short Course in Aerodynamics

Aerodynamics is the study of how air flows over and around a moving object—such as an airplane—and how airflow affects the moving object. Take a piece of 8½-by-11-inch paper, hold it about 6 feet above the ground, and drop it.

No matter if you hold the paper flat or by one edge, the paper will flutter and rock as it falls to the ground. It won't fall the same way twice, and you will have no control over the way it travels.

Next, carefully make sharp, ¼-inch accordion folds along one of the long edges of the paper, stopping when you reach the center. Staple or tape the folds together at the ends. The folded section of the paper is the "leading edge," or nose, and the opposite section is the "trailing edge," or tail.

Hold the paper by the tail about 6 feet high, and drop it. The paper falls much faster now. In fact, it swoops almost straight down. Can you guess why?

The paper falls faster when folded because the extra weight along one edge allows it to slip through the air. The heaviest part of the paper, the nose, falls first.

Now alter your sheet of paper again. With the folds underneath the paper, make a slight upward curve on the paper's trailing edge (Step 3). You can do this with your thumb and forefinger or by scraping the trailing edge across the edge of a table.

Can you guess how the paper will travel this time? Hold the paper by the tail about 6 feet high and drop it. Your paper travels in a roller-coaster fashion. This movement is caused by a property of aerodynamics called **lift.**

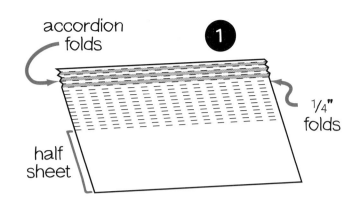

accordion folds

1

¼" folds

half sheet

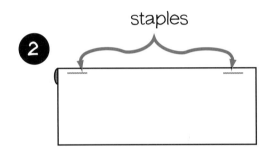

staples

2

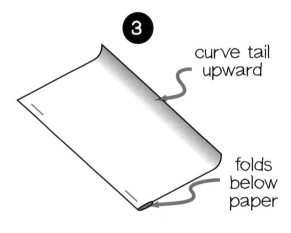

3

curve tail upward

folds below paper

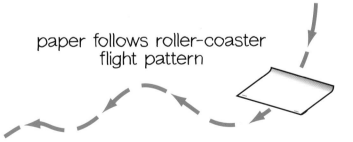

paper follows roller-coaster flight pattern

Lift, the upward force that opposes the pull of gravity, is created by a difference in air pressure above and below a surface, such as the wing of an airplane. The shape of a wing creates lift as the wing moves forward because the air pressure under the wing is greater than the air pressure above the wing.

To see an example of lift, fold a small sheet of paper—4 by 11 inches is good—in half and gently curve one section. Holding the paper by the flat surface, blow across the top of it.

Were you surprised when the paper moved upward as you blew across it? A scientist named Daniel Bernoulli discovered that air pressure falls when air speeds up.

When you blew across your wing, you increased the speed at which air passed over the paper, producing a low-pressure area above it. At the same time, the air pressure below the wing remained constant. Since air moves from higher pressure areas to lower pressure areas, the air below your wing moved upward with enough force to lift the paper.

Airplane designers use special lines called **streamlines** to show how air moves around objects. Look at the streamlines to the right. The typical airplane wing is designed to create lift. Because the top of the wing is curved, air moving over it has farther to travel than the air moving under it. The principles of aerodynamics require air moving over the wing to arrive at the trailing edge at the same time as air moving under the wing. So air passing over the curve must travel faster than the air passing below the wing. As a result, air pressure above the wing decreases. The higher pressure under the wing pushes the wing upward.

The position of a wing in relation to the air flowing past it is called the

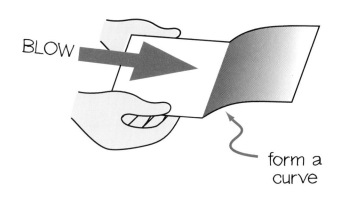

BLOW

form a curve

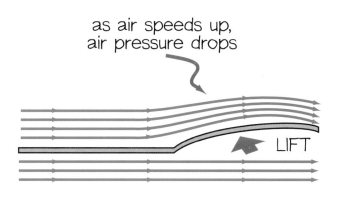

as air speeds up, air pressure drops

LIFT

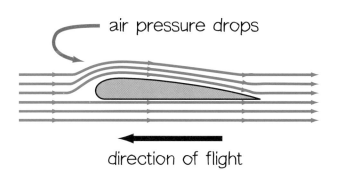

air pressure drops

direction of flight

angle of attack. A low angle of attack means a wing is tilted at a slight angle toward the flow of air. A high angle of attack means the wing is tilted at a high angle toward the flow of air.

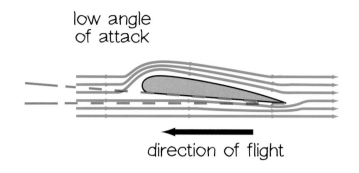

low angle of attack

direction of flight

A basic rule of physics is that for every action there is an equal and opposite reaction. When air hits an airplane wing, the air changes direction (action), and the wing moves upward (reaction). The higher the angle of attack of an airplane wing, the more the air changes direction, and the more the wing moves upward.

A higher angle of attack, then, causes greater lift. But air cannot flow smoothly around a wing positioned at too high an angle of attack. The air forms eddies, or swirls, which create **drag,** a force that slows the wing's forward motion. A wing set at a very high angle of attack can encounter so much drag that the wing will **stall** and fall downward. With a lower angle of attack, a wing cuts more smoothly through the air.

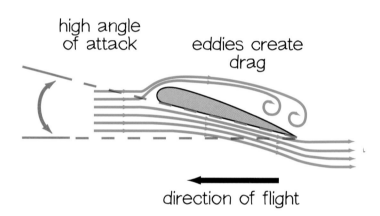

high angle of attack

eddies create drag

direction of flight

With all of this in mind, take another look at your paper from Step 3 on page 8. The upward curve on the trailing edge of your paper causes air to pass faster under the trailing edge and pressure to decrease below the trailing edge. The force of lift pushes the trailing edge down. The trailing edge drops, increasing the paper's angle of attack, pushing the nose upward, and creating more lift under the main portion of it.

Movable flaps found at the trailing edge of many airplane wings are called **elevators.** Elevators—just like the curve on your wing's trailing edge—affect an airplane's angle of attack. When elevators are raised, the nose, or front, of an airplane moves upward in

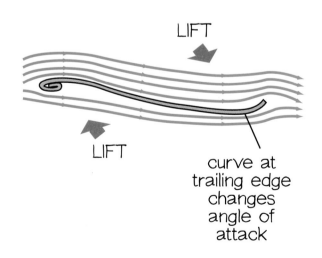

LIFT

LIFT

curve at trailing edge changes angle of attack

How roller-coaster flight happens

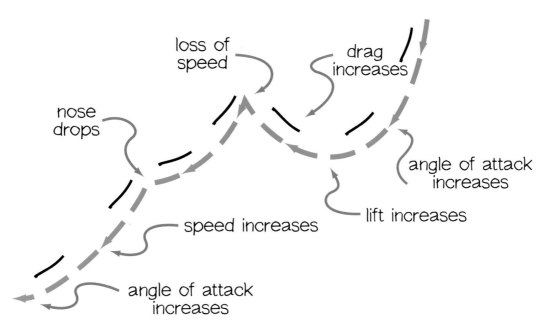

loss of speed

drag increases

nose drops

angle of attack increases

lift increases

speed increases

angle of attack increases

flight—just as your wing did. When elevators are lowered, the nose of a plane moves downward. This up and down motion of the nose is called **pitch.**

Other surfaces that can be moved to affect flight are **ailerons** and **rudders.** Like elevators, they cause air flowing past to change direction, and the plane reacts by moving in the direction opposite the airflow. Ailerons (usually found on the trailing edge of a wing) control the plane's **roll**—its side-to-side motion. Rudders (usually found on the trailing edge of a vertical fin) control **yaw**—the plane's left and right turning action.

When you release your paper, it picks up speed. Air flowing over the rear pushes down on the elevator, increasing the paper's angle of attack. The high angle of attack causes greater lift but more drag. The paper slows and the nose falls downward, creating a lower angle of attack. At this angle, drag decreases and the paper's speed increases again. Airflow

pitch

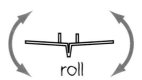

roll

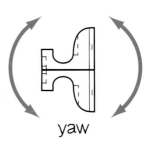

yaw

increases over the elevator, pushing it down. The paper climbs again—creating a roller-coaster effect that continues until it lands.

Fly your paper again. This time, lessen the curve (elevator) on the trailing edge and launch the paper forward rather than just dropping it. Adjust the curve and the launch speed until you get an even flight, without the roller-coaster effect.

Your paper will fly more evenly, but it probably rolls from side to side. You can control this wobbling motion by turning the single wing into an airplane with two wings.

Fold your paper in half to create a **keel.** Then create wings by folding the two sides back over the keel (Step 4). Give the wings a slight V shape, called a **dihedral** (Step 5).

Staple or tape the keel so that it stays closed. The keel and dihedral help keep the force of lift equal beneath both wings. This balance makes the plane more stable and helps prevent unwanted side-to-side roll.

Uncurl the trailing edges of the wings and cut two flaps as shown in Step 6. These flaps will be the plane's elevators. You now have a "Flying Wing" paper airplane. Flying Wings are aircraft that are all wing—with no real body. They also have no separate tail structure.

Make sure your plane's wings are flat—not warped in any way. Launch the plane and adjust the elevators until you get a smooth flight. If your plane flies in a circle with one side higher than the other, bend the elevator upward on the high side. If your wing stalls because it flies with its nose too high, bend the elevators slightly downward. Keep adjusting the elevators until the plane flies straight and level.

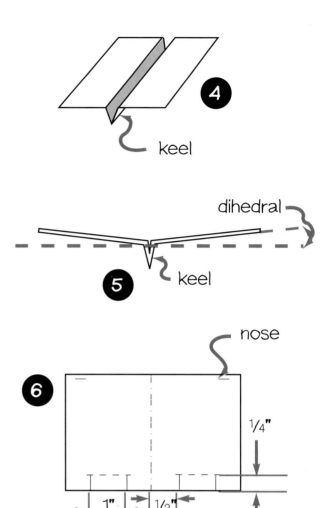

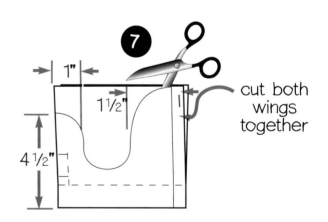

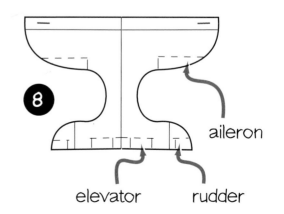

Now turn your Flying Wing into an airplane with a more complete set of controls. Fold your Flying Wing in half and make the cuts shown in Step 7. When you unfold it, you'll have an airplane that looks like the one in Step 8. Next, cut ailerons into the wings and fold and cut rudders into the tail. All cuts should be ¼ inch deep.

Adjust the elevators, ailerons, and rudders so your airplane flies straight ahead and smoothly downward. Change only one set of controls at a time so you can see how each affects your plane's flight. The time you spend experimenting now will be valuable later as you build and launch more complicated airplanes.

Adjust the controls on your airplane so it will make a **coordinated turn** to the right. A coordinated turn means the airplane turns with a slight rolling motion, not with a sideways skid. First check to see that your airplane's controls are set for straight and even flight. Now, looking at your airplane from its tail, turn both rudders slightly to the right. The right aileron should also be bent up slightly. Since lift decreases in a turn as the aircraft rolls away from level flight, bend up the elevators slightly to increase the wings' angle of attack. The controls should be bent as shown in Step 9.

Launch your airplane in a slight roll—that is, with the right wing

down. Adjust the controls until your airplane makes a slow, steady coordinated turn to the right. When you're done, try reversing the ailerons and rudders so that your airplane makes a slow coordinated turn to the left.

To make your plane do a loop, bend up the elevators sharply. Launch the plane quickly and at a high angle of attack. If your plane is adjusted properly, it will climb rapidly, then continue to fly upward into a loop. The flight will

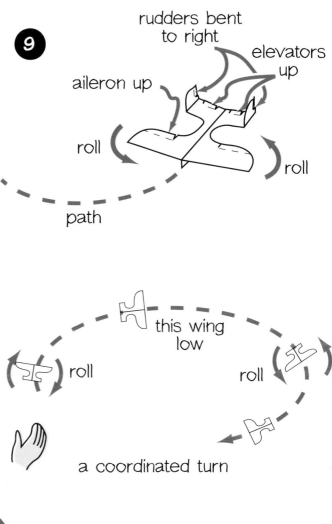

9 rudders bent to right
elevators up
aileron up
roll
roll
path

this wing low
roll
roll

a coordinated turn

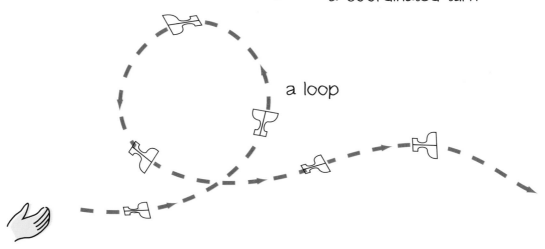

a loop

end in a series of roller-coaster ups and downs caused by the upward position of the elevators.

Each time you adjust the controls and launch your airplane, you are learning how to influence its flight. With your new knowledge of aerodynamics, you are on your way to becoming a good paper airplane pilot!

FLYING TECHNIQUES

All of the airplanes in this book are **gliders**—that is, non-motorized aircraft. They depend on the power of a launch, as well as gravity, for flying. While gravity would seem to work against flight, it helps a glider gain speed, which creates lift.

A good launch is essential to good flight. You must launch your airplane with the right speed, direction, and angle of attack.

If your paper airplane has a keel, hold the keel between your fingers for the launch. If your airplane doesn't have a keel, hold it near the nose, which is usually the strongest part of the plane. As you launch your airplane, follow all the way through with your hand. Release the plane with your fingers pointing in the direction of flight.

If you launch the airplane too slowly, it will fall without generating enough speed or lift for flight. If you launch it too fast, there will be too much lift, and the plane will climb steeply. Then it will stall or slow down until it begins to fall, speed up again, and repeat the pattern—moving in a roller-coaster fashion.

The angle of attack is as important as speed in beginning a flight. If the angle of attack is too low at launch, the airplane will dive until it picks up speed and lift forces the nose upward

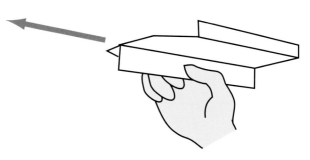

launch with a keel

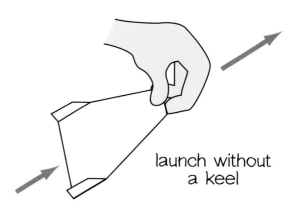

launch without a keel

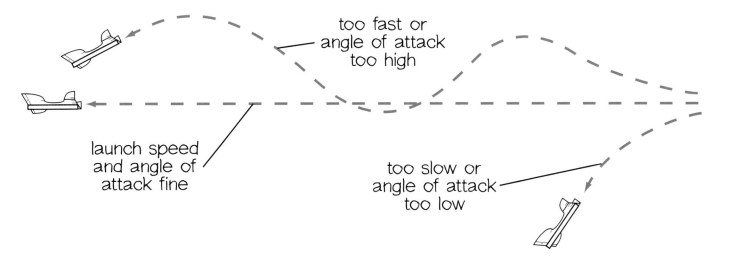

too fast or
angle of attack
too high

launch speed
and angle of
attack fine

too slow or
angle of attack
too low

again—unless the airplane hits the ground first. When the angle of attack is too high, the airplane will climb steeply, stall, fall, pick up speed, climb, and stall again until it finally lands. When the angle of attack and launch speed are correct, the airplane will glide smoothly downward until it lands.

The angle of attack and launch speed needed for smooth flight vary from airplane to airplane. The speed and angle of your launch will also depend on where you're flying your plane: indoors or outdoors, in a small room or in a large room (like a gym with high ceilings).

If you want your plane to make turns, launch it with one wing lower than the other to create a slight roll. If you have problems getting your paper airplane to fly smoothly, you may need to add **ballast**—more weight. Attach one or more small paper clips to the nose of your airplane at the keel.

Outdoors, wind speed and **turbulence** (swirling air currents) will affect your flights. Stronger and larger paper airplanes are best for outdoor flight. The best flying comes on days with light to calm winds. On these days, leaves may rustle, but tree branches will stay still.

Launching a paper airplane *into* the wind will increase its **relative flying speed**—that is, its speed compared to the air it's moving through—and it will gain altitude more rapidly. If you are launching your airplane *with* the wind, you must give it extra launching speed so it will have enough relative flying speed to generate lift. In general, launching with the wind will give you a smoother flight path. Experiment with each airplane to determine what works best.

If your airplane lands in a tree or another hard-to-reach place, leave it there. If the wind doesn't eventually bring the plane down, you can make another plane in just a few minutes. Don't get hurt trying to retrieve your airplane.

Your flying techniques will be different for outdoor and indoor flying, large planes and small planes, differently shaped airplanes, and different wind conditions. The best way to learn all the variables is to fly, fly, and fly! Like many things, flying paper airplanes is 10 percent knowledge and 90 percent practice and experience. Good flying and happy landings!

IMPROVED DART

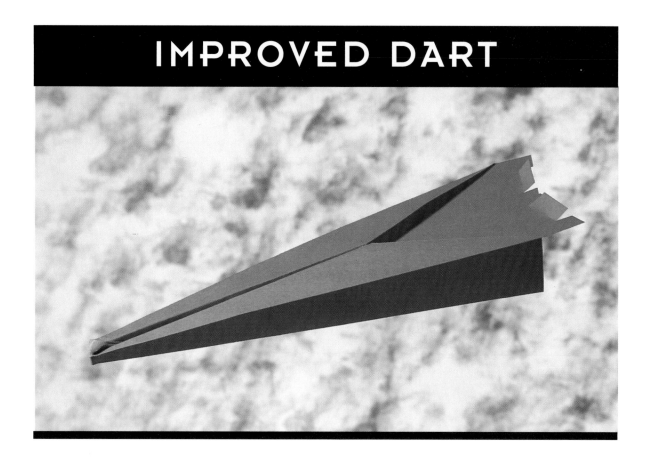

The Dart is the first paper airplane that many of us make. It generally flies like a dart—nose heavy.

   With the addition of some simple controls, the Dart airplane can be improved and made to glide farther and more predictably. I think you will be surprised at what a good flyer the dart can be!

1 Begin by folding an 8½-by-11-inch paper in half lengthwise (Fold 1). Crease the fold sharply.

2 Unfold the paper and pull the top corners inward, aligning the top edges with the crease (Folds 2 and 3).

3 Then fold the new edges over (Folds 4 and 5). Again, the edges of the paper should line up with the center crease.

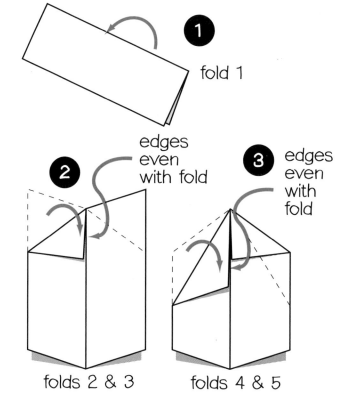

1 fold 1

2 edges even with fold

folds 2 & 3

3 edges even with fold

folds 4 & 5

4 Next, fold about 1 inch of the nose over (Fold 6). This gives the nose a safe blunt shape and reinforces it so it can withstand the knocks and bangs of hard landings.

5 Now turn your paper over. Fold the outside edges inward and align them with the center fold (Folds 7 and 8).

6 Turn the paper over and refold the plane along the center, so it is folded in half. Grasp the center fold and pull up on the sides. Now you have a keel and two wings. Place a short piece of tape across the top of the wings to hold them together, or staple the keel shut near the nose.

    This is a conventional Dart airplane. Test fly it. Your dart should fly a path curved downward.

7 You can quickly improve the Dart's flight characteristics by adding some controls. First cut two elevators into the tail, about ¼ inch deep and 1 inch wide. Bend them upward slightly. Your airplane should now look like the one in the diagram. Note the shape the wings and keel make when viewed from the nose—like the letter T.

Your Improved Dart should fly slightly nose high and more slowly than before. The elevators force the tail down in flight, creating a higher angle of attack and greater lift.

    This Improved Dart is, in fact, a long slender Flying Wing. You could even call the elevators **elevons,** because they have the duties of both elevator and aileron. The Improved Dart will easily fly straight, but it will only turn slowly and cannot make sharp loops.

    You might experiment with the Improved Dart's turning capabilities by cutting a small rudder into the rear of

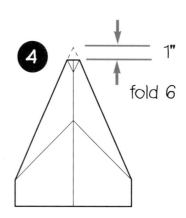

fold 6

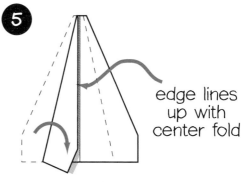

folds 7 & 8
(plane turned over)

edge lines up with center fold

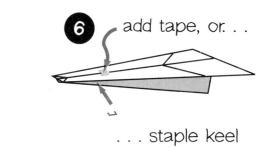

add tape, or . . .
. . . staple keel

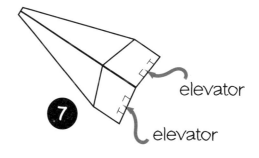

elevator

elevator

the keel. Bend it very slightly. Because the rudder is positioned below the wing, it turns and rolls the airplane at the same time, automatically forcing a coordinated turn.

FLYING VALENTINE

The Flying Valentine is a heart-shaped airplane. Its curved wingtips create dihedral necessary for stability. This airplane is fast but somewhat tricky to fly and adjust.

1 Begin your construction by aligning the top edge of an 8½-by-11-inch paper with the right edge to make a diagonal fold (Fold 1).

2 Then bring the top point across (Fold 2).

3 Next, fold the airplane in half lengthwise, with the other folds on the inside (Fold 3).

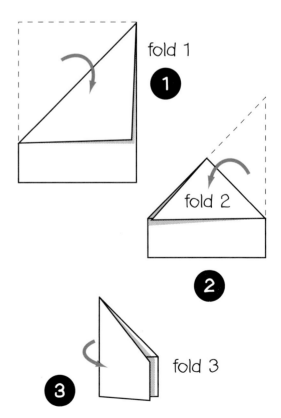

4 Now fold the nose over ¾ inch (Fold 4).

5 Fold the airplane in half again, then fold back the left wing along the line marked by an A (Fold 5).

6 Turn the airplane over and fold the right wing along Line B (Fold 6). Your airplane now has a keel. The wings should come to a point at the nose.

7 With the Flying Valentine folded in half, cut the wing's trailing edge to make the heart shape it will have when unfolded. Cut both wings and the keel at the same time.

8 Cut the two elevons in the trailing edge of the wing. They should be ¾-inch wide and ¼-inch deep.

9 Use your fingers to curl the wingtips upward, as shown. Add one or two paper clips to the nose of the keel for ballast.

The Flying Valentine is sensitive to adjustments. If you have problems, make sure that all of the folds are creased sharply. Add or subtract paper clips and adjust the elevons. With patience, this airplane will make good straight flights. The unusual shape looks good in the air—especially when made with red paper on Valentine's Day!

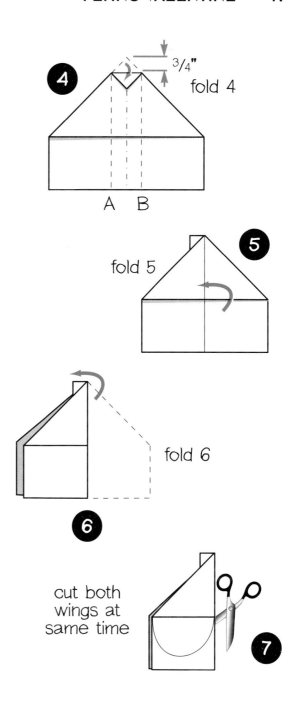

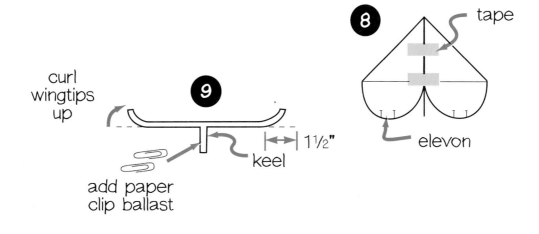

TRACTOR

When I discovered the Tractor as a child in elementary school, it became my favorite airplane because it was short, tough, and stubby—like a farm tractor.

I once flew a Tractor over a three-story school building on a windy day! This airplane is a steady flyer and can take lots of abuse.

1 As you did with the Flying Valentine, begin by aligning the top edge of an 8½-by-11-inch piece of paper with the right edge (Fold 1).

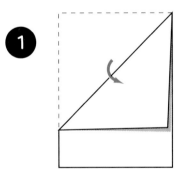

fold 1

2 Make Fold 2.

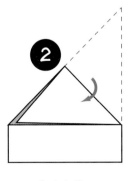

fold 2

3 Fold the airplane in half lengthwise (Fold 3).

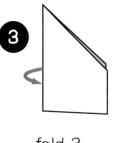

fold 3

4 Then fold the nose over until it touches the bottom of Folds 1 and 2, aligning the point with the center fold. The thickness of this airplane's nose gives it ballast.

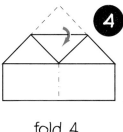

fold 4

5 Form a keel by making Folds 5 and 6. Staple and tape the keel tight together.

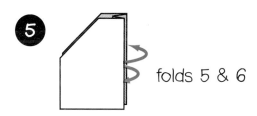

folds 5 & 6

6 Form two fins at the edges of the wings by making Folds 7 and 8.

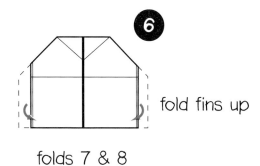

fold fins up

folds 7 & 8

7 Now make four ¼-inch cuts to form elevons on the tail and two ¼-inch cuts at the ends of the fins to form rudders.

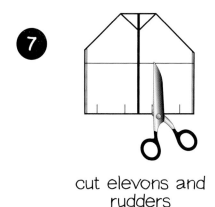

cut elevons and rudders

8 Tape the left edge of the front fold to the left fin as shown. Your airplane should look like the completed plane in the diagram.

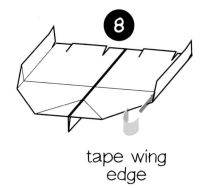

tape wing edge

9 Bend the elevons up slightly to give the aircraft a slight upward pitch. Leave the rudders straight for your first flight, and check to see that the wings are level and not warped in any way.

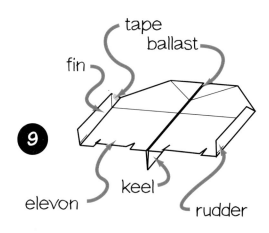

10 Try a flight. If your airplane won't fly smoothly, try adjusting the nose ballast. If the nose seems light, add a paper clip or two. If the nose seems too heavy, do Fold 4 again—but make the fold shorter to lengthen the wing and decrease the ballast.

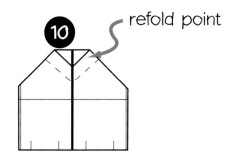

11 Now adjust the controls for a right-hand turn. The two elevons at the trailing edge of the wing do double duty as elevators and ailerons. When the elevons are positioned together, either up or down, they control the pitch of the airplane. If one elevon is in the up position and the other is down, they control the aircraft's roll.

Bend the right elevon slightly higher than the left and turn both rudders to the right. You may have to adjust the controls several times to get a smooth turn. Now make a left turn.

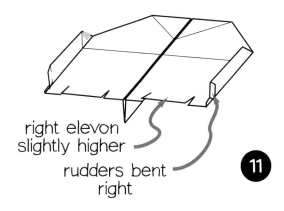

right elevon
slightly higher

rudders bent
right

11

12 Finally, adjust the controls for aerobatic flight, such as a loop. Bend both elevons upward and launch your plane at a steep angle. Because this airplane is short and has a fairly narrow wing span, it can perform aerobatic maneuvers well.

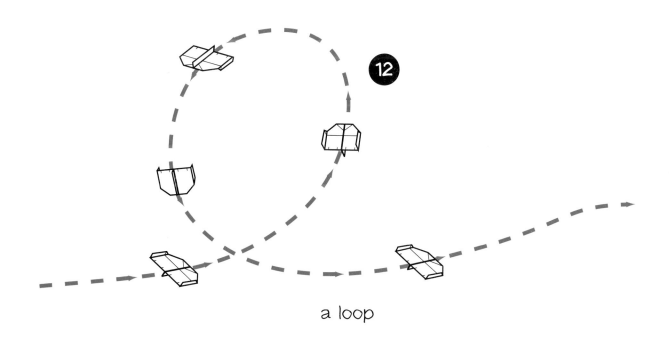

a loop

Barnstable-West Barnstable
School Library
West Barnstable, MA 02668

FLYING PANCAKE

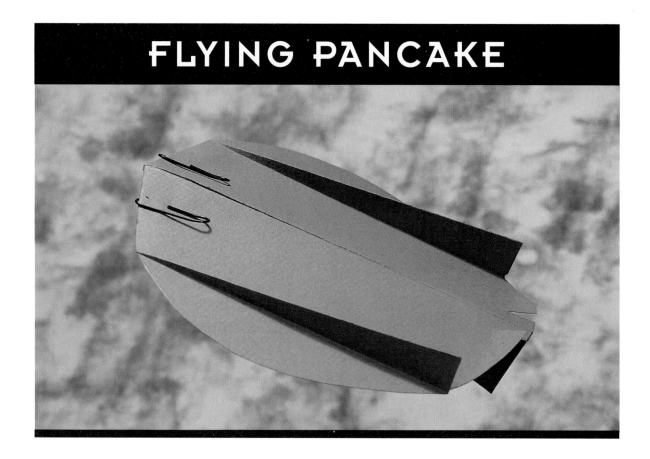

After World War II, the U.S. Air Force experimented with several unusual-shaped airplanes—including Flying Wings. The Air Force even built a circular Flying Wing, which they nicknamed the Flying Pancake.

This paper version of the Flying Pancake is quite a good flyer. It sports two fins and a tapered keel.

1 Begin by folding a piece of 8½-by-11-inch paper in half widthwise.

2 Unfold the paper and line up the crease with the center line shown on the template on the opposite page. Trace the pattern onto your sheet of paper. Lines show where folds go on the flaps attached to the nose, but you may choose not to draw them on your paper.

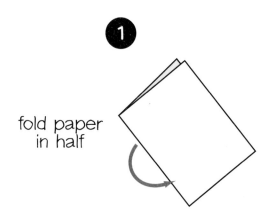

1

fold paper in half

inches

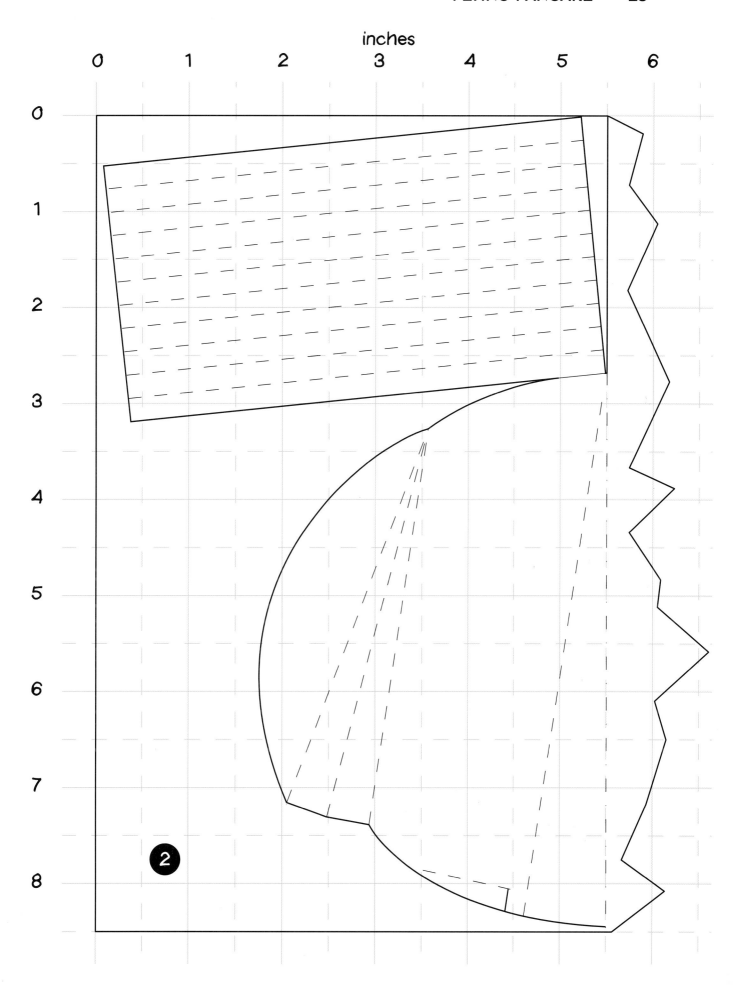

3 Fold the paper in half again, and cut along the solid lines. You will be cutting both the left and right sides at the same time.

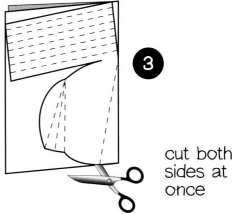

cut both sides at once

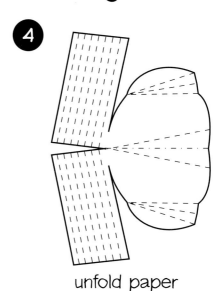

4 Unfold the paper and add fold and cut lines on the right side to create a mirror image of the left.

unfold paper

5 Fold the airplane so the keel points down and both fins point up.

fins folded up

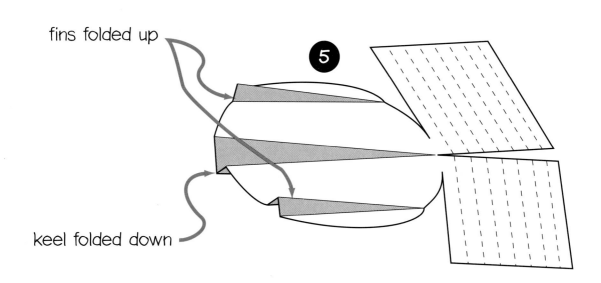

keel folded down

6 Tape or staple the fins and keel closed. Cut the elevons and bend them upward. Roll ¼-inch folds into the flaps attached to the nose.

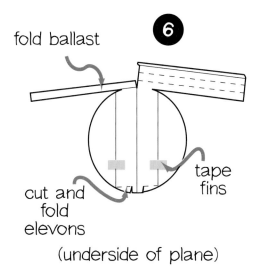

fold ballast

6

tape fins

cut and fold elevons

(underside of plane)

7 Fold these rolls under the nose for ballast and tape or paper clip them flat.

With the elevons bent slightly upward, launch your aircraft. You may need to add more ballast in the form of paper clips.

Because the airplane is all wing, it generates a lot of lift and needs quite a lot of ballast to fly well. Add and subtract paper clips and adjust the elevons until you achieve a smooth flight.

If you bend the end of the keel slightly, it will act like a rudder and help the plane make smooth, gentle turns. The plane will even perform loops when the elevons are properly adjusted and the amount of ballast is perfect.

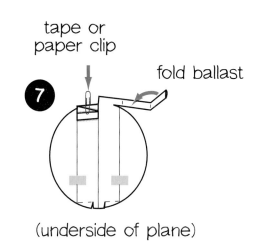

tape or paper clip

7

fold ballast

(underside of plane)

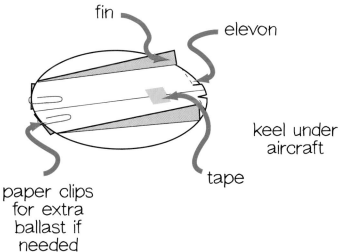

fin

elevon

keel under aircraft

tape

paper clips for extra ballast if needed

FLYING SHAMROCK

This unusual paper airplane is shaped like a shamrock! Made with green paper, it's perfect for flying on St. Patrick's Day.

Based on the shape of a real shamrock, the stem is the airplane's nose, the two leaves opposite each other are wings, and the single leaf above the stem is the tail. The Flying Shamrock uses a fairly large keel as a rudder. This airplane also has a main spar—a support beam—which makes the wings stronger.

1 Begin by cutting off 2 inches from the bottom of an 8½-by-11-inch sheet of paper, leaving your paper 8½ by 9 inches. Set the 2-inch strip aside.

2 Now fold the paper in half widthwise and trace the left wing (shown in the template on the opposite page) onto your sheet of paper.

inches

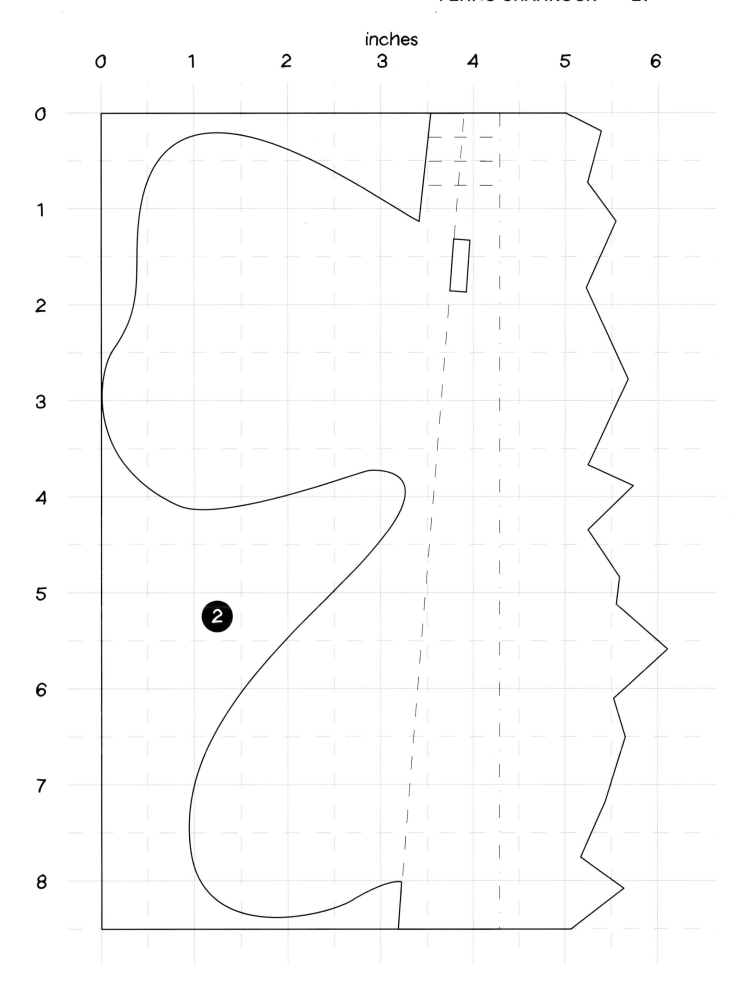

3 Using the left wing as a guide, cut out both wings at the same time. You will need a razor blade or a utility knife to cut out the slot for the **spar.** Be sure to protect your work surface with an old magazine or cardboard.

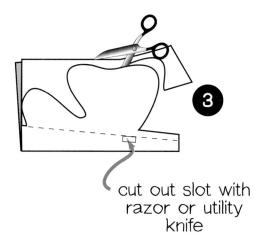

cut out slot with razor or utility knife

4 Unfold your paper. Draw the lines on the right wing, making it a mirror image of the left wing.

Fold over the nose section three times, making sure the ballast ends up on the underside of the airplane.

Fold the airplane in half at the center crease, then fold down the wings (Folds 2 and 3).

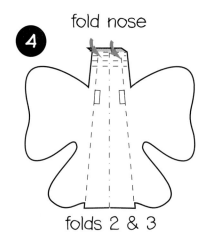

fold nose

folds 2 & 3

5 Open up the wings, and put a paper clip on the keel at the nose for ballast. Then tape or staple the keel together.

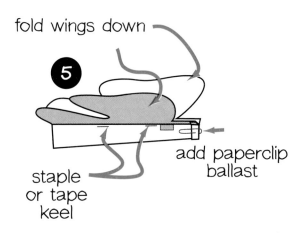

fold wings down

add paperclip ballast

staple or tape keel

6 Next, take the 2-inch strip of paper and fold it in ¼-inch strips to make a spar ¼ inch wide by 8½ inches long. Staple or tape the spar so that it stays folded tight.

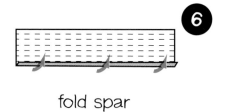

fold spar

7 Insert the spar through the slot in the keel, with the closed end forward. Tape the spar flat to the underside of the wing and trim the ends so they're even with the wing tips.

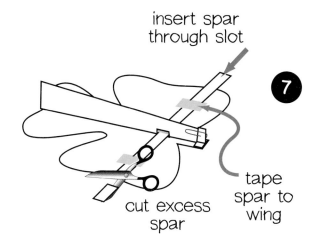

insert spar through slot

7

cut excess spar

tape spar to wing

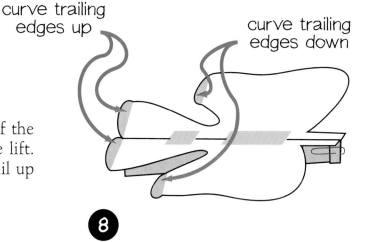

curve trailing edges up

curve trailing edges down

8 Finally, curve the trailing edges of the wings down slightly to get more lift. Curve the trailing edges of the tail up to raise the nose slightly in flight.

8

Test fly your airplane, adjusting the curve of the wings, tail, and the amount of ballast until you get straight, smooth flights. Bend the end of the keel to make your Flying Shamrock do turns.

OBLIQUE FLYING WING

Experiments in aerodynamics proved that a wing can fly at an oblique angle—not only perpendicular to the direction of flight. Airplane designers have used swept-back wings for years to help airplanes fly faster than the speed of sound. Wings with an angle less than 90 degrees in relation to the direction of flight allow air meeting the wing to "slide off" the leading edge. This reduces shock waves and the "sonic boom" caused by flying faster than the speed of sound.

This straight wing is stronger than a swept-back wing. And because the wing flies at an oblique angle to its line of flight, it still flies "swept back" to the air passing past it.

Because the Oblique Flying Wing is a simple glider, it cannot fly at a sharp angle; about 20 degrees is best.

1 Begin construction by laying out the cut and fold lines from the template on the opposite page to your 8½-by-11-inch paper. If you want to make a larger wing—one that uses the entire width of your paper—enlarge the template 130 percent with a photocopier.

Cut out the airplane, and discard the paper scraps.

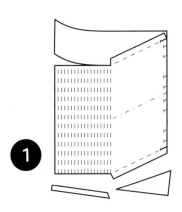

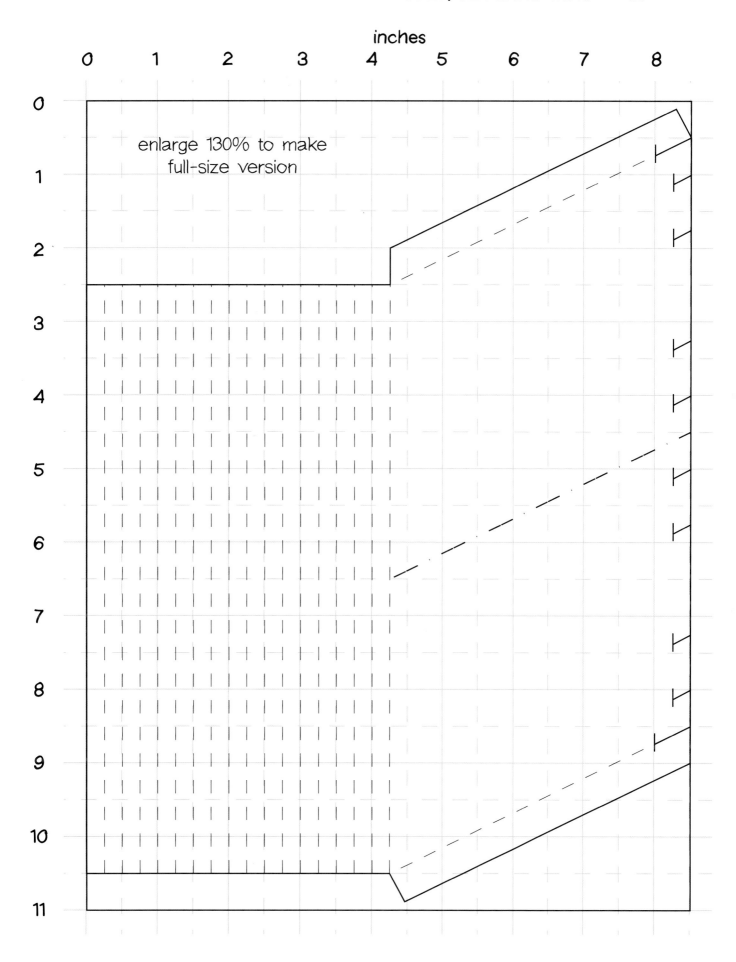

inches

enlarge 130% to make
full-size version

2 Next, make the ¼-inch accordion folds, creasing them tightly so they lay flat.

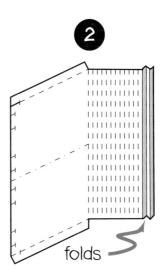

folds

3 Staple or tape the folds to the underside of the leading edge. When you do this, you will have extra paper from the accordion fold extending past the left side of the nose. Using your scissors, clip off this extra paper.

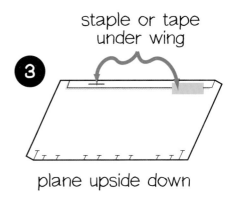

staple or tape
under wing

plane upside down

4 Now make the cuts for the elevators and ailerons as shown. Both surfaces are needed to control the oblique wing's tendency to turn right. Next, fold the fins up and make ¼-inch cuts at the back of the fold lines to form rudders.

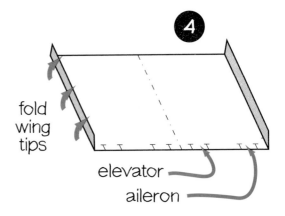

fold
wing
tips

elevator

aileron

5 Finally, make the preliminary control adjustments. Crease the center line so the wing tips form a total dihedral of ½ inch. The elevators should be bent up at about a 45-degree angle. The aileron on the right wing should be bent down. The aileron on the left wing should be bent up.

Test fly the airplane and adjust the controls for a straight and level flight. Since this aircraft has no keel, grasp the aircraft near the center by the leading edge. If the wing needs more ballast, add paper clips on the leading edge at the center of the wing.

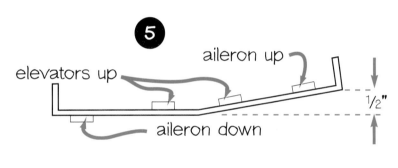

looking down nose of
plane

Moving the ballast left along the wing will help compensate for the airplane's tendency to turn right. To send the wing into a gradual right turn, set the ailerons to the "neutral" position—neither bent up or down—which will allow it to follow its natural course. Left turns are more difficult. You might achieve a gentle left turn by using the rudders at the ends of the fins and making larger adjustments to the ailerons. Also try decreasing the dihedral.

Experiment to see how well you can maneuver this airplane. You can also try to make an oblique wing with a "left-hand" angle by reversing the angles in the instructions. If you modify the pattern from page 33, you can experiment with wings made with a greater or lesser angle.

STEALTH WING

The real Stealth Bomber is a flying wing. The plane has no vertical fin to control yaw. Instead, the airplane has sets of ailerons that control both yaw and roll. The ailerons on the right wing create drag to make the airplane yaw to the right. The ailerons on the left wing create drag for turning left.

This paper version of the Stealth Bomber has a small keel at the nose of the airplane to help control yaw. The keel also helps to keep the airplane from skidding sideways in the air. As on the Stealth Bomber, the ailerons—the outermost flaps—on this Stealth Wing control roll as well as yaw. This paper airplane, like the real Stealth Bomber, has a swept-back wing.

1 Begin by drawing cut and fold lines on your paper. Note that the wings will be cut separately and must be "mirror images" of each other. You can make the airplane by tracing the template onto your paper at the size shown. You can also make a larger Stealth Wing by enlarging the template 130 percent on a photocopier.

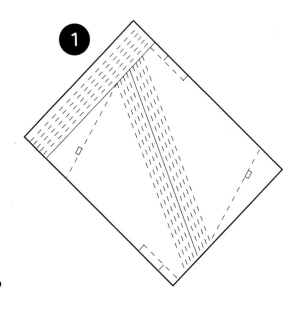

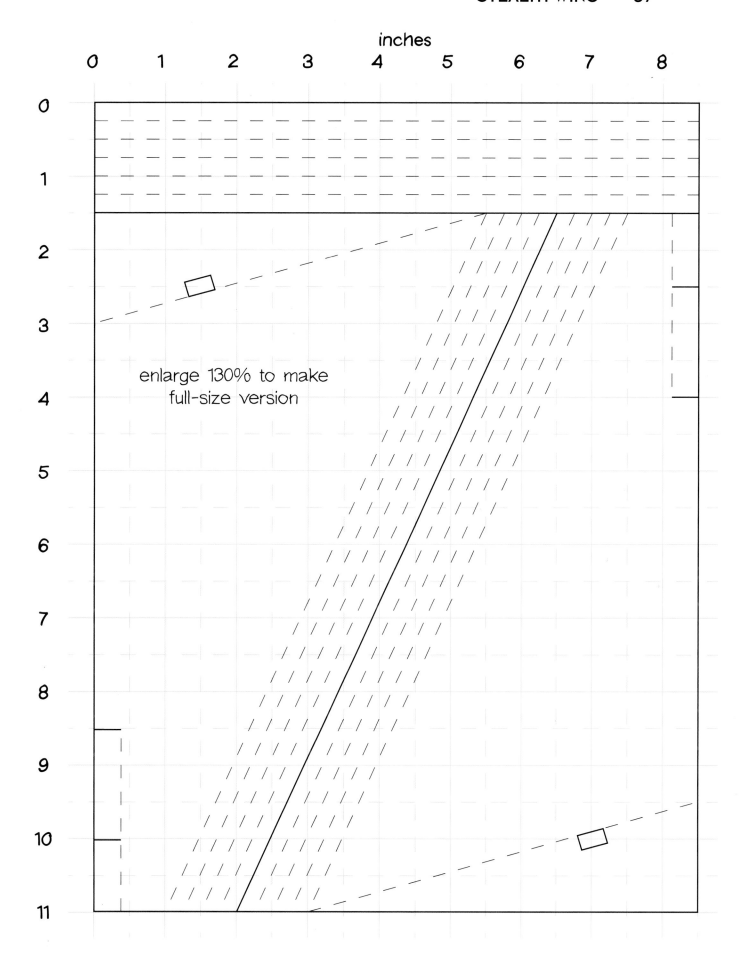

inches

enlarge 130% to make
full-size version

2 Cut off the spar piece and lay it aside. Cut the wings apart, then make ⅜-inch cuts for the ailerons and elevators at the outside tip of each wing. Cut slots in the keel for the spar.

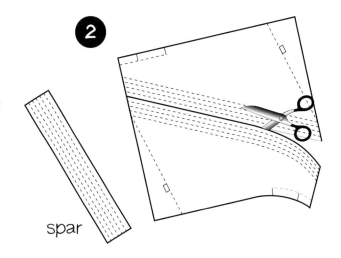

3 Fold the leading edges beneath both wings. Staple or tape the folds flat against the underside of the wings.

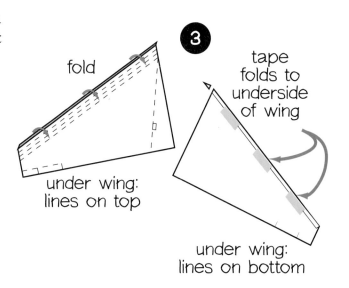

4 Next, fold the keels under the wings. Fasten the two keels together with tape at all of the edges. Place a 3-inch piece of tape on top of the airplane, across the centerline of the keel.

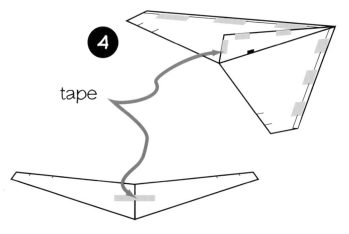

5 Fold and tape the spar.

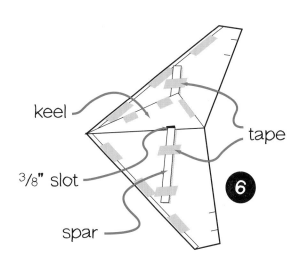

5 fold spar

6 Thread the spar through its slot in the keel, keeping the open flap toward the back of the wings, then tuck the ends under the leading edge folds. Tape the spar to the wings.

7 Add paper clips as ballast, slipping them over the leading edge of the wing, close to the keel. Bend both elevators upward and test fly your airplane. Bend the aileron upward on the right wing for a right turn or upward on the left wing for a left turn.

keel

tape

³/₈" slot

6

spar

Balance is critical to the flight of the Stealth Wing. To fine-tune the balance, slide a paper clip along a wing to help get straight and level flight. You may have to curve the trailing edge of the wing that flies higher upward slightly to decrease the lift on that wing. Because this airplane is all wing with lots of lift, the wings should have as little curve as possible. If your elevators cannot keep the nose up with the extra ballast needed to make steady flights, make a second set of elevators just inside the first set.

If you make this airplane out of black paper, it will closely resemble the real Stealth Bomber—especially in flight!

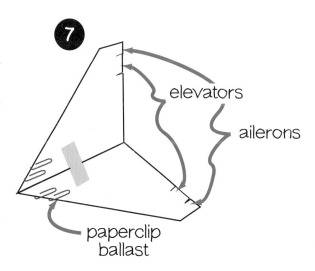

7

elevators

ailerons

paperclip ballast

PAPER HOVERCRAFT

Here is a paper airplane that flies less than an inch above the floor. Hovercraft are more accurately described as vehicles, but—like airplanes—they do leave the ground.

A hovercraft moves forward while "floating" very close to the ground. The vehicle is supported by a cushion of air that has a higher pressure than the air all around it. This bubble of air is trapped under the deck by side skirts, and it lifts the craft until air leaking from under the skirts reduces the pressure.

This Paper Hovercraft is the "ram" type. That is, as the craft moves forward, air is rammed into the front and is trapped there, increasing the pressure under the craft. The craft rises until air leaking from under the skirts causes it to descend.

The craft rises, descends, and then stabilizes just above the floor. The Paper Hovercraft finally slows down until the air pressure is no longer high enough to hold it above the ground. This hovercraft will "fly" 20 to 30 feet or more across a smooth floor.

inches

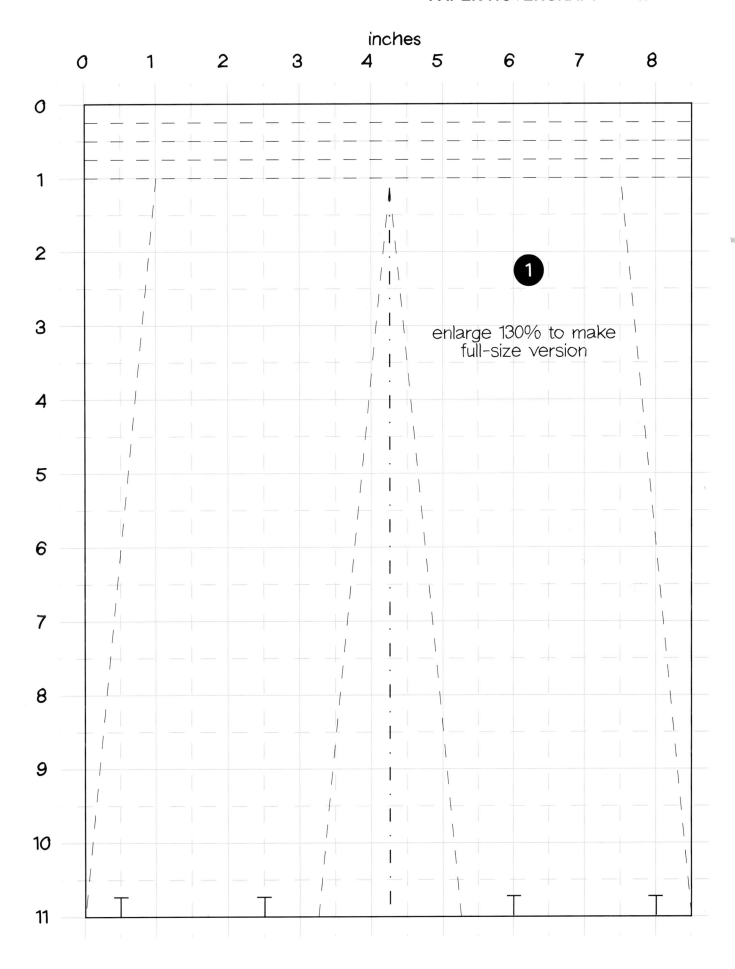

enlarge 130% to make
full-size version

1 Begin construction by laying out the fold lines according to the diagram on the previous page. You can make the airplane by tracing the template onto your paper at the size shown. You can also make a larger Paper Hovercraft by enlarging the template 130 percent on a photocopier.

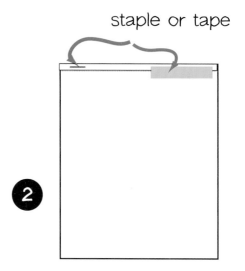

staple or tape

2 Make the ¼-inch folds first, stapling or taping them flat under the leading edge of the deck.

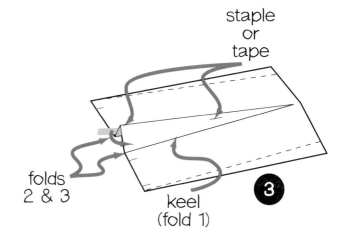

staple
or
tape

3 Now make Folds 1, 2, and 3 so the fin rises above the deck. Be sure to stop the crease just short of the front folds. Staple the fin shut, or affix a piece of tape across the seam on the underside of the plane. Make ¼-inch cuts for the elevators.

folds
2 & 3

keel
(fold 1)

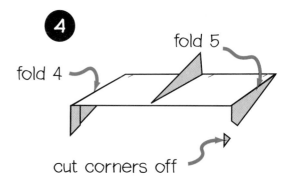

fold 4

fold 5

4 Make Folds 4 and 5, then cut off the front corners of the skirts so they won't get caught on slight obstructions protruding from the ground.

cut corners off

5 Next, break a paper clip in half by bending the wire back and forth until it breaks. Discard one half and bend the other into a hook.

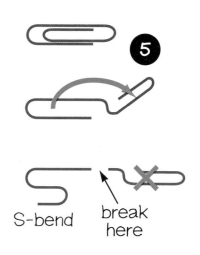

6 Poke the hook through the deck so the bottom wraps around the folds at the front of the craft. Use a narrow strip of tape to keep the hook in position.

S-bend   break here

7 Lastly, place two large paper clips at the nose for ballast. Holding the rear of the fin between your thumb and index finger (and keeping the craft ½ inch above the floor), attach a rubber band to the hook. Stretch the rubber band slightly, then release the fin to launch your Paper Hovercraft.

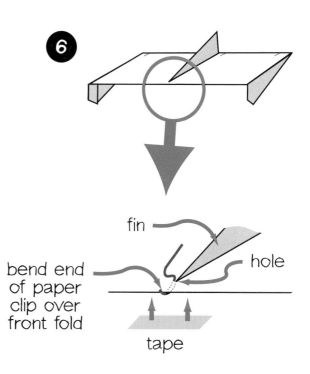

fin

bend end of paper clip over front fold

hole

tape

If the nose tends to rise and causes the craft to fly more than 1 or 2 inches above the ground, try adding more ballast or reducing your launch speed. Strive for a smooth, straight path above the floor. If your craft rises on one side only, slide the ballast toward that side. You will be surprised at how fast and far this craft can go. Gentle turns can be made by bending the rear of the fin to form a rudder. Remember, aircraft control is the mark of a good pilot!

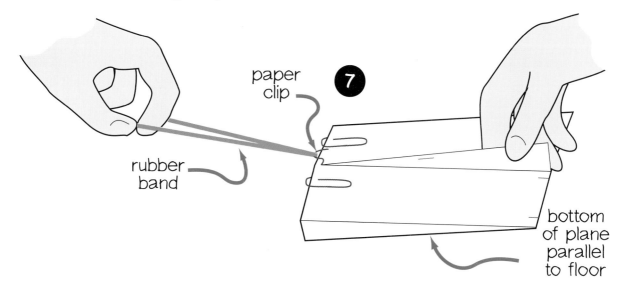

paper clip

rubber band

bottom of plane parallel to floor

ULTRALIGHT

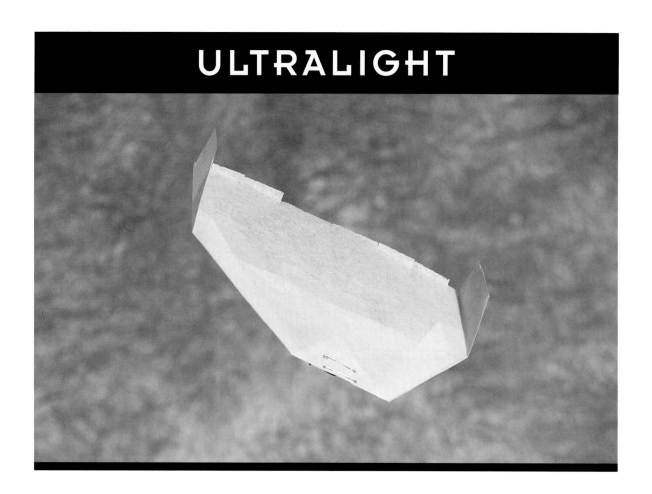

The Ultralight is both light and small. It is built with just a quarter sheet of tissue paper and is so light that staples are used for ballast. The Ultralight flies slowly and—because of its small size—can be flown in a small area. I have seen this airplane make three complete 360-degree turns when launched from a height of six feet.

1 Begin constructing your Ultralight by cutting a piece of tissue paper—such as that used in packing gifts—into a rectangle 4¼ inches by 5½ inches. Make Fold 1 on the centerline, then unfold the paper and lay it flat, crease side up.

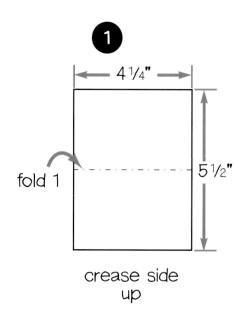

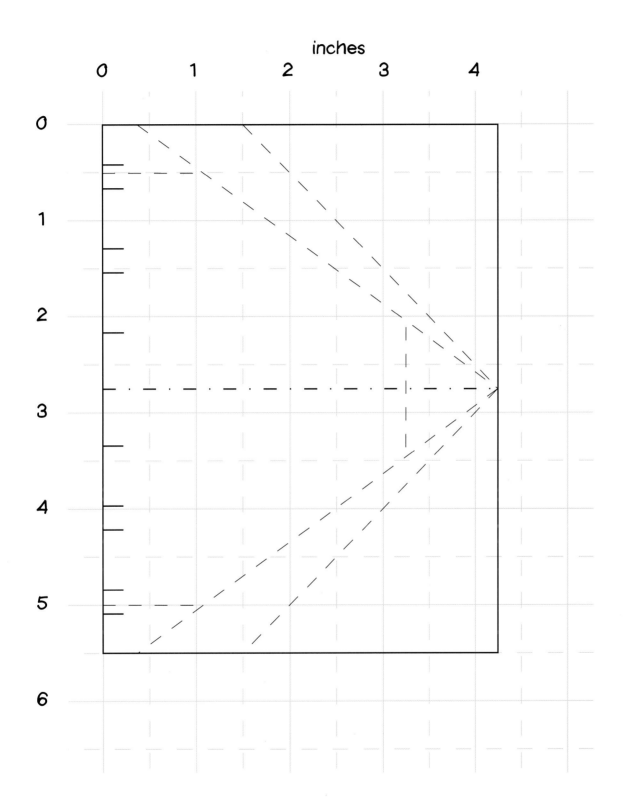

2 Next, make Folds 2 and 3, pulling the top edges to the center crease.

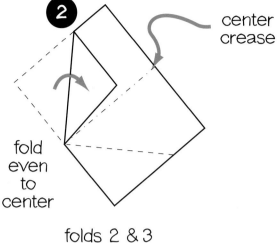

folds 2 & 3

3 Then fold the outer edges inward again (Folds 4 and 5), from a line starting ⅜ inch from the trailing edge to the tip of the nose.

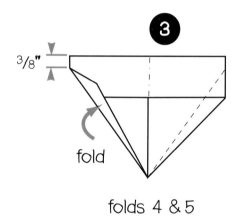

folds 4 & 5

4 Make Fold 6, bringing the nose inward an inch, then crease all folds tightly. Tape the folds flat. To keep this airplane as light as possible, use the smallest piece of tape that will secure each fold.

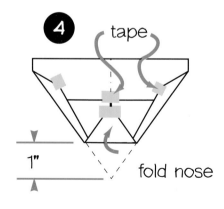

fold 6

5 Turn your paper over and fold up the wingtips ½ inch (Folds 7 and 8).

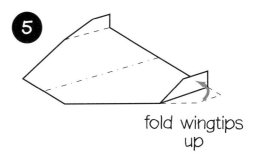

fold wingtips
up

folds 7 & 8

6 Cut ⅛-inch deep ailerons and elevators into the trailing edge of the wings. Also make ⅛-inch cuts into the fins to form rudders. Make sure that the widths of the controls are the same on both sides of the airplane.

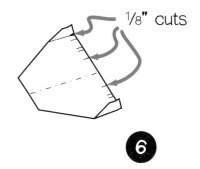

⅛" cuts

7 Bend the elevators up and test fly your airplane. Since this Ultralight has no keel, you will have to hold it by the nose. Be sure that there is a little dihedral toward the rear of the plane. You will probably need to add nose ballast in the form of staples. The lighter the airplane, the slower it will fly.

To get the plane to make a loop, bend both elevators and ailerons up. Hold the airplane in front of you—fins pointing away from you. Now give the airplane a sharp upward flip. It should make a tight loop and "roller coaster" its way down to the floor. If you are careful and quick, you can even catch it at the end of the loop.

   Smooth coordinated turns are possible if you adjust the rudders and ailerons together. Because this airplane flies slowly, be patient and make adjustments carefully to get the best flights out of your plane.

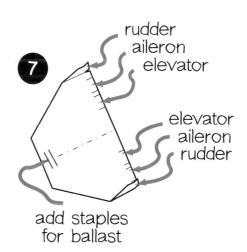

rudder
aileron
elevator

elevator
aileron
rudder

add staples
for ballast

DRAGONFLY

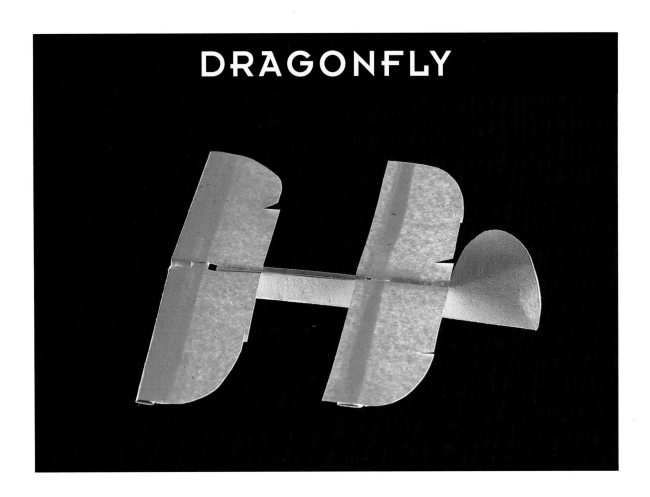

The Dragonfly is a biplane because it has two wings. Unlike the usual biplane, which has one wing above the other, the Dragonfly is a tandem biplane with one wing behind the other. Both wings provide lift. The front wing has ailerons to control roll, while the rear wing has elevators that control pitch. Several famous airplanes use the tandem biplane design, including the Quicky, designed by renowned airplane designer Burt Rutan, and a French plane called "The Flea."

1 Begin constructing your Dragonfly by cutting off two 1½-inch pieces from the bottom of an 8½-by-11 inch sheet of paper. These will become the spars. Lay them aside. Then fold your paper in half lengthwise, unfold it, and trace the cut and fold lines for the right side of the airplane—using the template on the opposite page.

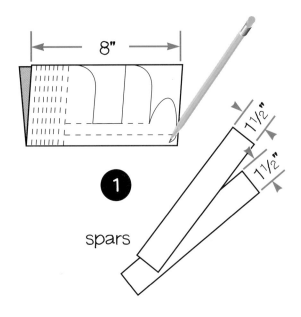

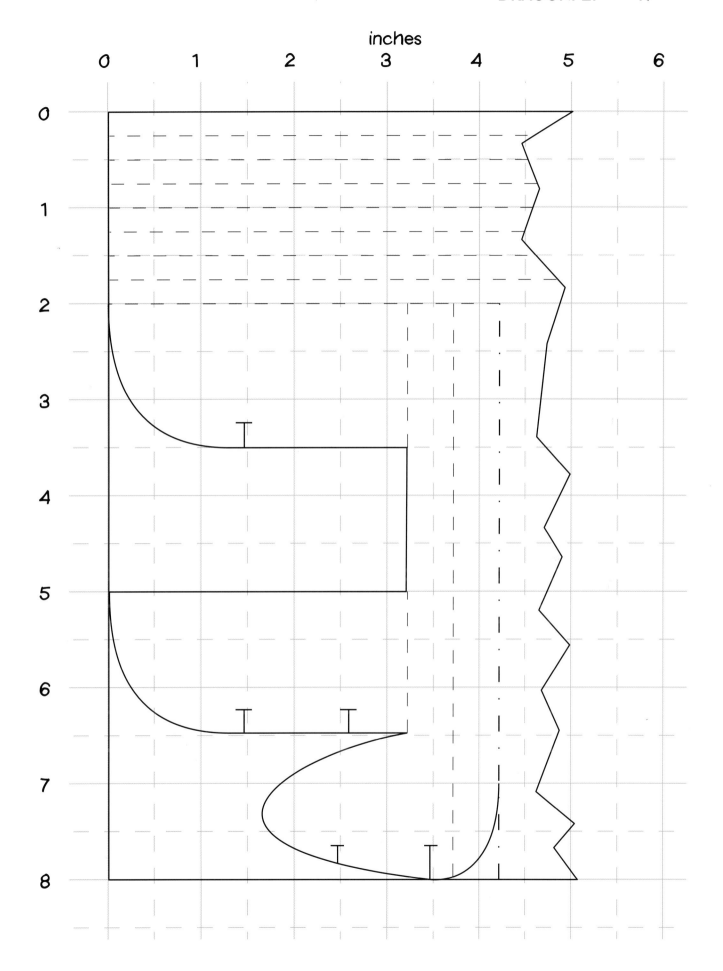

2 Next, cut out your airplane and discard any waste paper.

Make the folds for the leading edge. Staple or tape the folds flat against the underside of the wing.

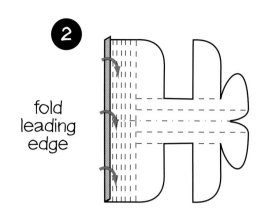

2

fold
leading
edge

3 Mark both spars for ⅛-inch wide folds. Fold and tape the spars tight.

3

mark and fold
spars

4 Make Fold 1.

4

center
fold
(fold 1)

5 On the airplane body, make Folds 2 and 3. Then flip the airplane over and make Folds 4 and 5. Note that the keel has four layers of paper to give it extra stiffness.

5

folds 2
& 3

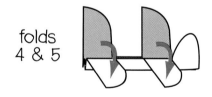

folds
4 & 5

6 Staple or tape the keel closed. Tape all edges of the vertical fin together.

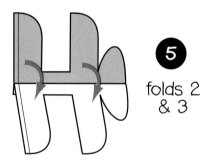

tape

6

staple

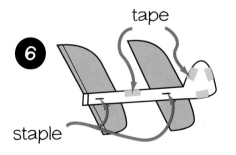

7 Use a sharp knife or a razor blade to cut the spar slots for both wings. Be sure to protect your work surface with a piece of cardboard or an old magazine. Note that the spar for the front wing fits just behind the front folds, and that the spar for the rear wing fits just behind the leading edge.

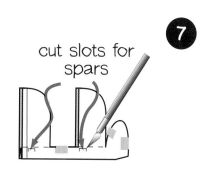

cut slots for spars

7

8 Insert each spar through its slot with the open edge to the rear of the wing. Tape the spars flat to the undersides of the wings, then trim them even with the ends of the wings.

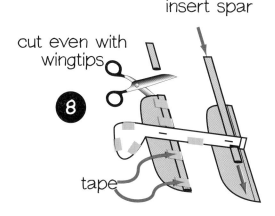

insert spar

cut even with wingtips

8

tape

9 Add paper clips as ballast to the front of the keel. Next, make ¼-inch cuts at the ends of the front wings for ailerons, and on the rear wing near the vertical fin for elevators. Then form the rudder. Make a ⅜-inch cut near the bottom of the tail. One inch above the bottom cut, make a ³⁄₁₆-inch cut into the tail. The cuts are different lengths because of the tail's shape.

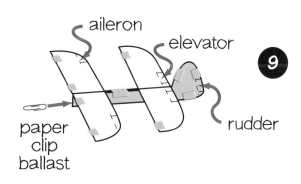

aileron

elevator

9

paper clip ballast

rudder

Flying the Dragonfly is similar to flying most of the airplanes in this book. Adjust the controls and the ballast until your plane flies smoothly and straight. If the airplane rolls, bend down the trailing edge of the front wing on the side that flies low, increasing its curve.

This airplane will make maneuvers if you adjust the controls the same way as you have for the other airplanes in this book. Because the wings are fairly narrow, the Dragonfly must fly faster than airplanes with wider wings so it can generate enough lift to stay airborne. You will find that the airplane will react faster to adjustments in the control surfaces because air passes over them at a higher rate of speed. Adjust the controls carefully to get the maneuver you want.

VERI-EZE

Burt Rutan, who designed the Quicky described in the last chapter, also created the real Veri-Eze. The Veri-Eze is a type of airplane called a canard, which has small front wings and large rear wings.

On the Veri-Eze, the front wing has elevators and is set at a slightly higher angle of attack than the rear wing. When the aircraft is flying at a steep angle—close to stalling—the front wing stalls first and lowers the plane's nose, preventing the large rear wing from stalling. This feature makes the Veri-Eze a safe plane to fly.

The rear wing has ailerons to control roll. Two vertical fins at the wing tips control yaw. The fuselage (body) of this airplane is triangular, made separately from the wings.

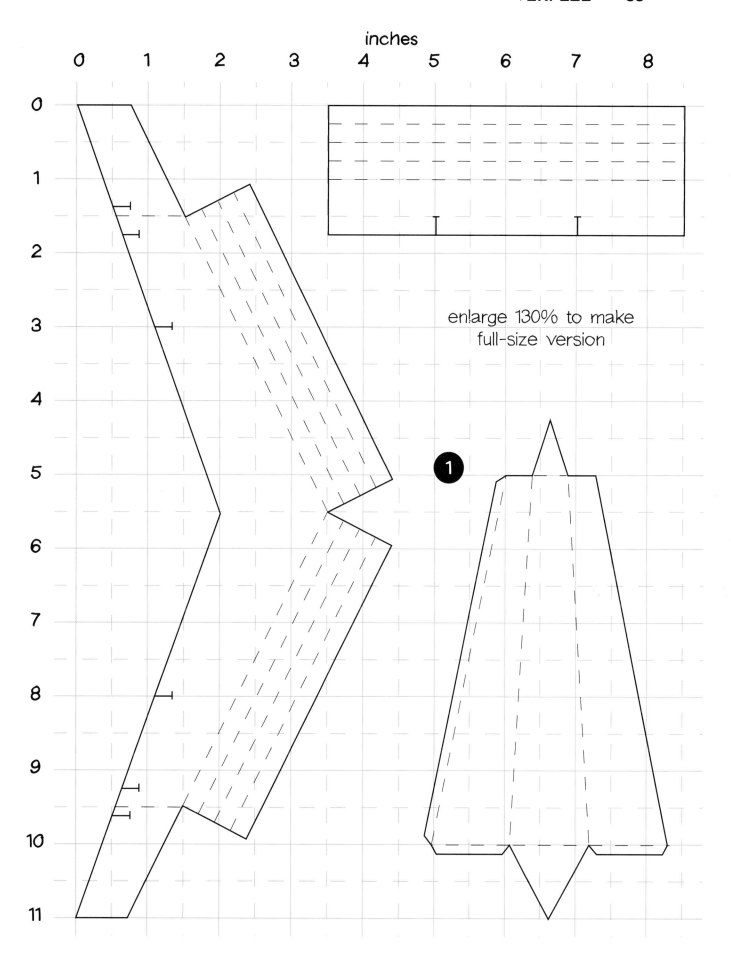

inches

enlarge 130% to make
full-size version

1 Trace the pattern from page 53. To make a larger airplane, enlarge the pattern 130 percent on a photocopier.

2 Cut out all pieces—the two wings and the fuselage—and discard the extra paper. Using Diagram 2 as a guide, cut two triangular flaps into the fuselage sides to form a slot for mounting the front wing. Fold these flaps inward. Next, cut apart the flaps on top of the fuselage and fold them upward. These top flaps will be taped to the top of the wing when it is attached.

3 Also on the fuselage, cut slots for the rear wing.

Crease the leading and trailing end flaps, then fold the fuselage into its triangular shape. Fold the long fuselage tab over the seam and tape it flat. This is the bottom edge of the fuselage.

4 Fold the fuselage tail cap downward, and fold the ⅛-inch tabs over the cap. Tape the fuselage tail shut.

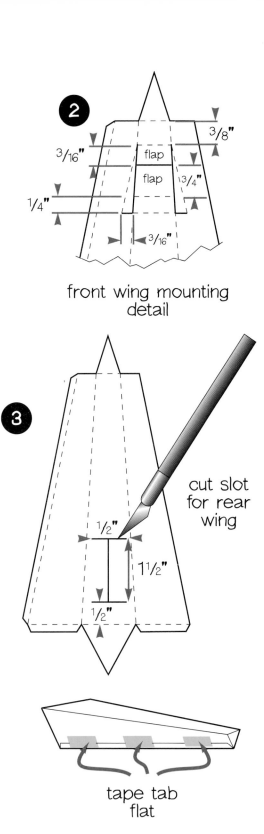

2

3/16″ 3/8″

flap

flap 3/4″

1/4″

3/16″

front wing mounting
detail

3

cut slot
for rear
wing

1/2″

1½″

1/2″

tape tab
flat

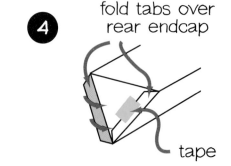

fold tabs over
rear endcap

4

tape

5 Bend the fuselage nose cap downward, until the point is even with the bottom angle of the fuselage. Fold the side flaps of the fuselage even with the nose cap and tape the nose shut.

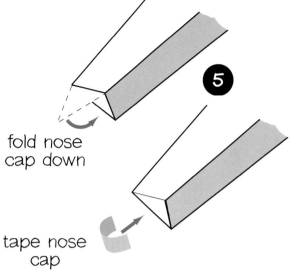

fold nose
cap down

tape nose
cap

6 Next, make the leading edge folds of both wings and staple or tape the folds flat to the underside of the wings.

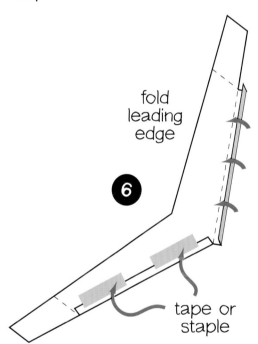

fold
leading
edge

tape or
staple

7 Fold the fins on the rear wing upward to form a 90-degree angle (Folds 1 and 2). Then crease the rear wing at the centerline (Fold 3) to give it a dihedral of ¾ inch. Make the rudder and aileron cuts ¼ inch deep.

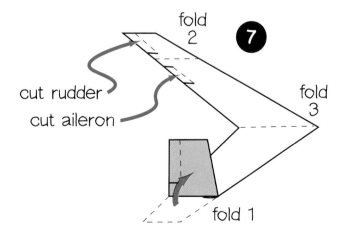

fold
2

cut rudder

cut aileron

fold
3

fold 1

8 Place the front wing under the flaps at the front of the fuselage. Tape the flaps to the front wing, and cut the elevators ¼ inch into the front wing.

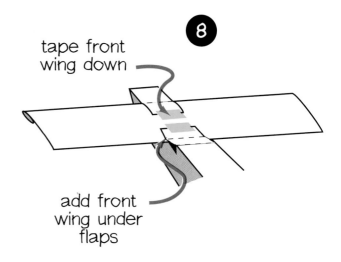

tape front
wing down

8

add front
wing under
flaps

9 Now tape the rear wing to the rear of the fuselage, fitting the point into the slot. The wing should be taped so the dihedral is even on both sides of the fuselage.

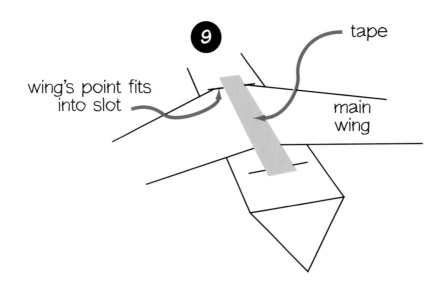

9

tape

wing's point fits
into slot

main
wing

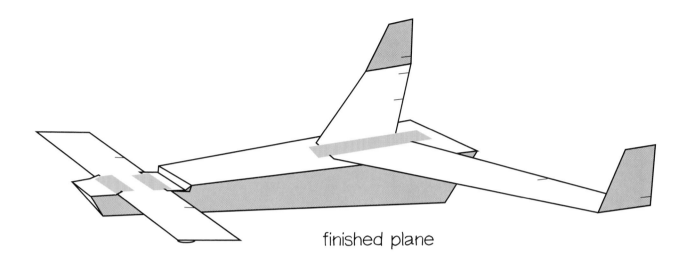

finished plane

The Veri-Eze is a steady, fast flyer. Like the Dragonfly, this airplane reacts to a small adjustment in the controls. Launch your airplane at a steep angle to try to force a stall. You should find that the nose will come down before the airplane stalls. The airplane will pick up speed and fly smoothly again.

You can adjust the ailerons and rudder for turns. Because the elevators are on the front wing, bending them down will force the airplane nose upward, while bending them up will force the nose downward.

Adjust the controls and ballast until you get a smooth, straight flight. If you need more ballast, add paper clips to the front wing near the fuselage. If your airplane rolls, use the ailerons on the rear wing to correct the roll.

LILIENTHAL GLIDER

This airplane is a scale model of the 1894–1895 Lilienthal Glider. Near the end of the 19th century, a German named Otto Lilienthal made the first controlled airplane flights. He flew his airplanes—a series of gliders—much like modern hang gliders. Lilienthal picked up the airplane, ran down a steep hill to gain speed, swung his legs up off the ground, and flew. By swinging his legs and body, Lilienthal found he could control pitch and roll.

Otto Lilienthal died in a flying accident in 1896, before he could carry out plans to experiment with powered flight. Lilienthal's ideas about airplane design were advanced for his day, and his findings encouraged others to carry on in the field of aviation.

This paper model of Lilienthal's glider has a main wing, a horizontal tail, and a vertical fin like most modern aircraft. The pilot (made of pipe cleaners in this model) can control the airplane by changing its balance.

inches

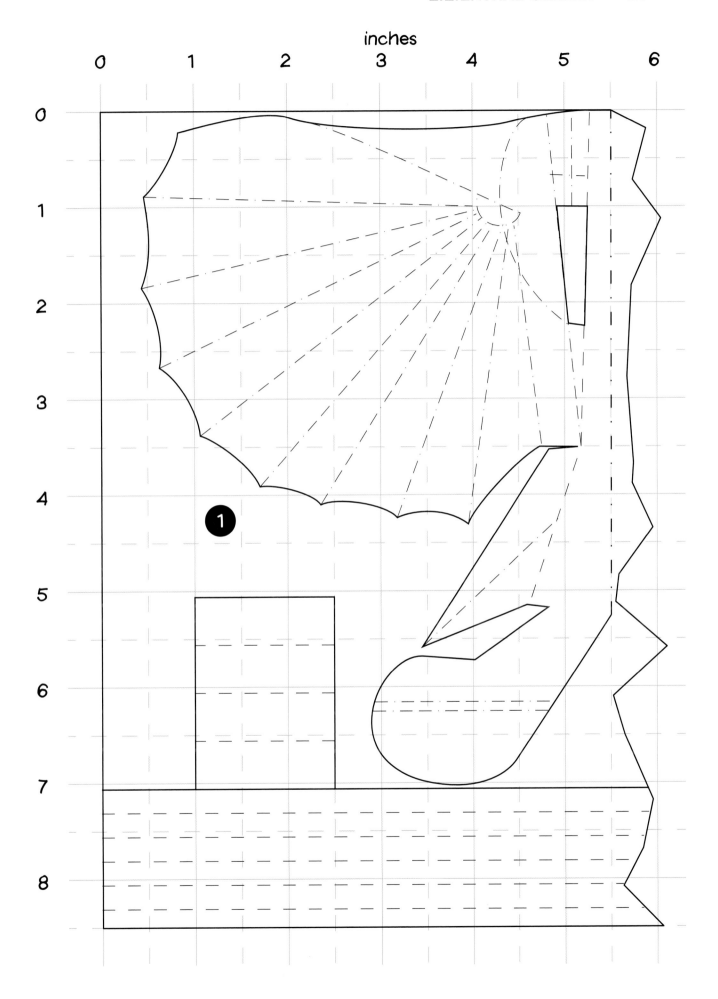

1 Fold your paper in half, then unfold it with the crease upward. Trace the left side of the airplane from the template on the previous page onto your paper. The lines with the dot-dashed pattern show where the real glider had a bamboo frame. Trace these lines onto your paper too.

2 Cut out the spar and keel brace and lay them aside. Fold your paper in half along the centerline, with the lines showing outside the crease. Cut out both sides of the airplane at the same time. Use a sharp knife to make the two cutouts near the center of the plane.

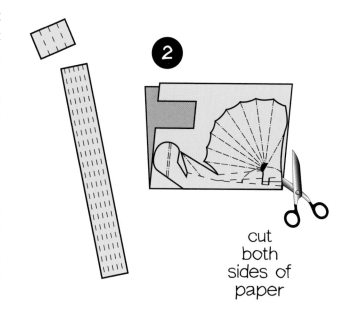

cut both sides of paper

3 Draw the special dot-dash lines on the right wing—making it a mirror image of the left wing. Darken all the special lines so they will look like a bamboo frame. If you turn the paper over and draw the lines with a lighter pencil, they will look like a frame seen through cloth. If you use a light tan or parchment-colored paper, the wings will look even more like cloth.

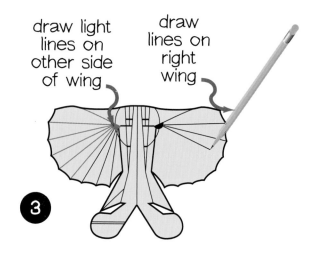

draw light lines on other side of wing

draw lines on right wing

4 Fold and crease the wings along each of the frame lines. The creases should be on top of the wing. With the creases, the paper will be curved and will look like cloth stretched over a frame.

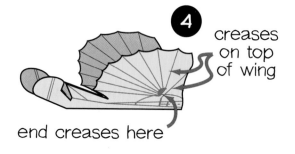

creases on top of wing

end creases here

5 Fold the plane along the centerline again. Fold the wings and tail surfaces down along the keel fold lines. Tape the keel together at these places: the cutouts, the vertical fin, across the keel at the wings' trailing and leading edges, and at the horizontal tail.

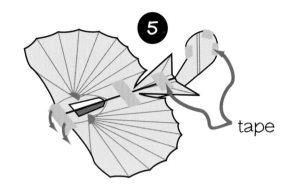

tape

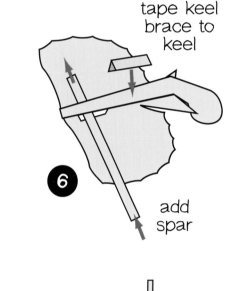

tape keel brace to keel

add spar

6 Fold the ³⁄₁₆-inch and ¼-inch folds in the spar and the ½-inch folds in the keel brace. Tape the spar flat. With the open flap to the rear, slide it under the wing, over the keel at the front of the two cutouts, and then under the other wing. Tape the spar to the underside of the wing so the wing takes a slight dihedral. Fold and tape the keel brace in place on the keel so the center of the brace is under the leading edge of the horizontal tail.

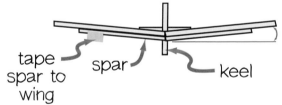

tape spar to wing

spar

keel

7 Cut eight pipe cleaners to a length of 4 inches. Insert them through the wing, four to each cutout.

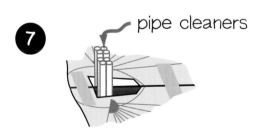

pipe cleaners

8 With about 1½ inch of the pipe cleaners above the wing, twist them to form the pilot's head and shoulders.

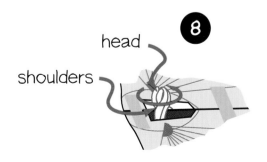

head

shoulders

9 Bend two of the pipe cleaners under the wing to form arms with elbows and hands. The hands should wrap around the front of the wing's spar.

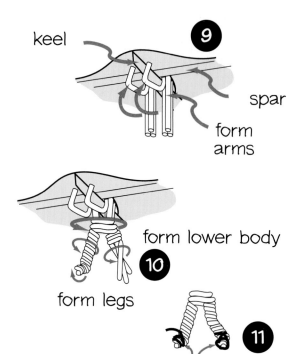

keel

9

spar

form arms

10 Twist the top part of the remaining six pipe cleaners to form the pilot's waist and lower body. Divide the remaining untwisted pipe cleaners into two groups of three each and twist them together to form legs. Bend each leg so that it has a knee and foot.

form lower body

10

form legs

11

solder ballast

11 Wrap a 1-inch piece of solder (or wire, if you don't have solder) around each foot to act as ballast. If you want your glider to look real spiffy, you can make paper clothes for your pilot.

flatten wings

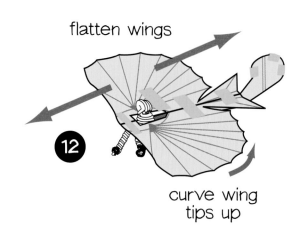

12 Flatten the wings by pulling gently on the leading and trailing edges of each. Curve the wing tips upward slightly.

12

curve wing tips up

Test fly the glider. If it dives toward the floor, bend the pilot's legs toward the rear of the aircraft. If the plane noses up, move the legs toward the nose. If the glider still noses up with the pilot's legs extended all the way forward, add more wire to the feet or flatten the wings even more. Most flights will have a gentle roller-coaster motion as the plane glides downward.

Make gentle turns by bending the pilot's legs slightly in the direction of the turn.

The Lilienthal Glider has a very limited range of speed. If the glider flies too slowly, it will stall and fall. If the glider flies too fast, it will nose up, stall, and fall. This problem was mostly likely the cause of Lilienthal's fatal crash.

THE SKY'S NOT THE LIMIT

The Lilienthal Glider recalls the earliest days of aviation. Perhaps the glider marks the beginning of your discovery of aviation and flight too. Where do you go from here?

You can start by reviewing the planes in this book. Modify them, make them larger or smaller, change the shape—even design your own airplanes. You now have a basic knowledge of aerodynamics and enough experience to get your own creations flying.

You could organize indoor and outdoor flying contests with other paper airplane pilots. Who can fly their airplane the farthest, the highest, or for the longest time? Whose plane performs the best aerobatic stunts?

Who can make the most accurate controlled flights? Choose a point on the ground and see whose plane lands closest. Try playing "paper airplane golf." A small ring placed on the ground or the floor can serve as the hole. The course can be as simple or as complicated as you choose.

You might want to read books about model gliders and model airplanes built from wood or plastic. Some model airplanes have engines and radio controls that allow them to fly like real airplanes. You can also learn to make kites and apply your knowledge of aerodynamics to kite flying.

You might even consider studying about and learning to fly real airplanes. The aerodynamic forces that enable paper airplanes to fly are no different from the forces that control space shuttles.

When aviation was new, people said, "The sky's the limit!" But with modern space travel, the sky is just a beginning. There's no limit to flight—not even the Earth's atmosphere! With your imagination and your desire to learn about flight, there are no limits to how far you can go in space and aviation, either.

GLOSSARY

aerodynamics: the study of forces acting on objects in motion through the air, such as airplanes

ailerons: movable surfaces at the trailing edge of an airplane's wing that control roll

angle of attack: the angle at which a wing meets the air flowing around it

ballast: extra weight placed on an airplane at particular spots to help it maintain steady flight

coordinated turn: a turn in which an airplane rolls slightly and turns at the same time, with one wing lower than the other

dihedral: the angle of an airplane's wing to its keel, fuselage, or opposite wing

drag: the friction of air passing around an airplane that slows the airplane down

elevons: control surfaces that take on the function of both elevators and ailerons

elevators: movable surfaces at the trailing edge of an aircraft that control pitch

fuselage: the body of an airplane

gliders: non-motorized aircraft

keel: the flat, vertical part that usually runs the entire length of the airplane, centered between the wings

lift: the upward force created when air flows past a wing

pitch: an airplane's movement in relation to its lateral axis; if an airplane changes pitch, its nose rises or falls

relative flying speed: the speed of an airplane in relation to the speed of the air flowing past it; the greater a plane's relative flying speed, the greater the force of lift acts on it

roll: an airplane's movement in relation to its longitudinal axis; when an airplane rolls, it tips to one side or the other

rudders: movable surfaces on a vertical surface that control yaw

spar: support beams that give strength to the wings of an airplane

stall: to reach a point at which lift is insufficient for maintaining flight

streamlines: lines that show how air flows around an object such as an airplane

turbulence: disruptions in airflow, particularly ones that cause a swirling motion in the air

yaw: the turning movement of an aircraft in relation to its vertical axis

745.592   Kelly, Emery J.
KEL
          Paper airplanes.

$23.93

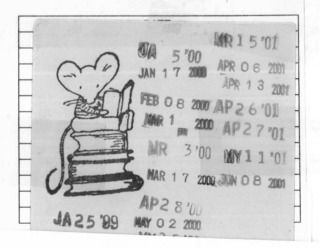

Barnstable-West Barnstable
School Library
West Barnstable, MA 02668

BAKER & TAYLOR